Problem Solving Made Easy

AGES 9-11

Author and Consultant
Sean McArdle

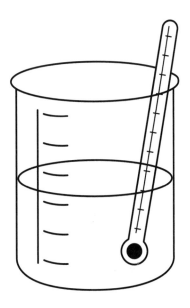

Certificate

Congratulations to

....
(write your name here)

for successfully
finishing this book.

GOOD JOB!

You're a star.

AGES 9-11

Key Stage 2

Date

....

Penguin
Random
House

Editors Jolyon Goddard, Arpita Nath
Art Editor Yamini Panwar
Senior Art Editor Ann Cannings
Art Director Martin Wilson
DTP Designer Anita Yadav
Producer, Pre-Production Nadine King
Producer Priscilla Reby
Managing Editor Soma B. Chowdhury
Managing Art Editor Ahlawat Gunjan

First published in Great Britain in 2016 by
Dorling Kindersley Limited
80 Strand, London WC2R 0RL
Copyright © 2016 Dorling Kindersley Limited
A Penguin Random House Company

10 9 8 7 6 5 4 3 2
002–285367–Jan/2016

A CIP catalogue record for this book is
available from the British Library.

ISBN 978-0-2412-2497-7

Printed and bound in China

A WORLD OF IDEAS:
SEE ALL THERE IS TO KNOW
www.dk.com

Contents

This chart lists all the topics in the book. When you complete each page, stick a star in the correct box. When you have finished the book, sign and date the certificate.

★ Time problems

How many hours are there between 22:00 and 02:00?

22:00 to 00:00 = 2 hours

00:00 to 02:00 = 2 hours

2 + 2 = 4 hours

4 hours

Poppy met Blake at the Natural History Museum at 14:30.
They spent three hours there. What time did they leave?

Chen's digital watch shows 11:10. It is, however, 26 minutes fast.
Calculate the actual time at that moment.

Idris and Monica decided to visit the National Gallery in London.
Monica arrived there at 16:05, whereas Idris arrived 40 minutes earlier.
What time did Idris get there?

Marcel only understands the 24-hour system for telling the time. He wants to watch a football match. The television guide says the match begins at 1.30 p.m., but he doesn't understand what time that is. Can you help Marcel by telling him what 1.30 p.m. is in the 24-hour system?

Arya thinks 16:20 is the same time as 6.20 p.m. Can you help Arya by telling her what 16:20 really is in the 12-hour system?

Dakota read in her history book that the Great Fire of London happened in the year MDCLXVI. Help Dakota write the year in numbers.

| 1666 |

M = 1000, D = 500, C = 100, L = 50, X =10, V = 5 and I = 1

1000 + 500 + 100 + 50 + 10 + 5 + 1

= 1666

Using Roman numerals, write the number that is 10 more than each of these.

V [ ]   VIII [ ]   XLV [ ]

Write each of these years using Roman numerals.

2014 [ ]   2002 [ ]   1918 [ ]

A farmer counted his two flocks of sheep one morning. One flock had DXII sheep and the other had D. How many sheep does the farmer have altogether? Write your answer in Roman numerals.

[ ] sheep

In her maths exam, Greta had to solve this sum and write the answer in Roman numerals. What should she have written?

MDI + MCL = [ ]

The year before last, the population of a small town was MDV. Last year, however, the population went down by DL. Calculate the new population of the town and write the answer in Roman numerals.

[ ]

The cost of laying a garden patio is £48 per square metre. If the area of the patio is 8 m², what will be the total cost of laying it?

| £384 |

40 x 8 = 320

8 x 8 = 64

320 + 64 = 384

Emerson's trip to France is going to cost him £660. He has, however, saved only a third of that amount so far. How much more money does Emerson need to save for his trip?

Lauren participated in a sponsored run for her favourite charity. She asked people to sponsor her 50 p for every kilometre she runs. Ten people sponsored her and she raised a total of £70. How many kilometres did Lauren run?

Four different coins make a total of 82 p. What are the coins?

Each month, Scarlett puts away a quarter of her wage as savings. If she earns £1 600 a month, how much money does she spend?

It costs Eddy £380 to get his car repaired at his local garage. A fifth of the cost is for new car parts and the rest goes towards labour charges. How much do the parts cost and how much does the labour cost?

Cost of parts   Cost of labour

Which decimal amount is the same as seven-eighths?

> $\frac{1}{8}$ = 0.125
>
> $\frac{7}{8}$ = 7 x 0.125
>
> = 0.875

0.875

At Clement Academy, maths lessons take up 0.2 of the school week. If a school week is 20 hours, how much time does the academy devote to subjects other than maths?

Three-fifths of £18 is spent on a cinema ticket and 0.4 of the remainder on sweets. How much money is left after buying the ticket and the sweets?

If 0.9 of a number is 63, what is the original number?

Akiko pays 20% tax on her monthly wage. If Akiko earns £1 680 a month, how much money will she have left after paying tax?

A bookshop owner adds three-tenths to the price of each book he sells to a customer. If a new book costs the customer £15.60, how much did it cost the bookshop owner?

The distance between Winchester and Walsall is 135 miles. Only 0.15 of the distance is motorway. What distance is not motorway?

In a class of 20 pupils, seven have blond hair. What percentage is that?

35%

Percentage means "of 100"

$20 = \frac{1}{5} \times 100$

$7 \times 5 = 35$

7 out of 20 = 35%

A mobile phone comes with 40 free apps already loaded. Five of these are quiz apps and four are music apps. What fraction of the free apps are neither quiz nor music apps?

apps

At a charity fundraiser, 1 000 lottery tickets are sold. The chance of winning with a ticket is 0.01. What is the maximum number of people who could win?

people

For their football album, Lou collected 46 football cards and Eve collected 34. What percentage of the total number of football cards did each collect?

Lou

Eve

An estate agent charges a commission of 1.25% of the selling price of each house. If a house is sold for £480 000, how much will the agent make as commission?

Alexander has rented out his house for £900 a month. At the end of the first month, he spent two-fifteenths of the rent he was paid on repairs and kept the rest as profit. How much profit did he make that month?

In one year, the price of petrol rose by 5%. If the original price was £1.20 per litre, what did it cost after the rise?

£1.26

5% of £1 = £0.05
5% of 20p = £0.01

1.20 + 0.05 + 0.01
= 1.26

Write the percentage equivalent of these fractions.

$\frac{9}{10}$ [ ] $\frac{4}{5}$ [ ] $\frac{7}{20}$ [ ]

Rowan practises for a marathon by running 12 km a day. A few days before the marathon, he increases the distance by 15%. Calculate the new distance Rowan runs.

[ ]

In a school with 1 400 pupils, 45% have French classes and the rest study German. How many study each language?

French [ ]   German [ ]

A teacher needs to mark 40 exercise books in one evening. After three hours, he has marked 0.7 of them. How many books still need to be marked?

[ ] exercise books

A restaurant expects each customer to pay a 15% tip on his or her bill. If a meal at the restaurant costs £45, how much tip will a customer be expected to pay?

[ ]

A doctor has 4 800 registered patients. Last year, however, only 1 920 patients visited her. What percentage did not visit her last year?

[ ]

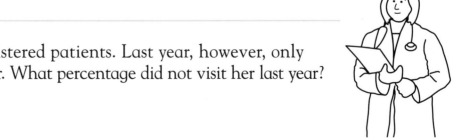

★ Ratio problems

A woodland has trees in the ratio of two oaks to seven elms. If there are 16 oak trees in the woodland, how many elm trees will be there?

| 56 | elms

oak:elms = 2:7
16 (oaks) = 8 x 2
so number of elms = 8 x 7
= 56

In a class of 30 children, six children bring packed lunches from home and the rest have school meals. What is the ratio of packed lunches to school meals? **Note:** Write the ratio as simply as possible.

The ratio of a school playground's length to its width is 5:4. If the area of the playground is 180 m², calculate its length and width.

Length [   ]   Width [   ]

In a packet of sweets, for every four red sweets there are two yellow sweets and one purple sweet. If the packet costs £1.12, how much does each type of sweet contribute towards the total cost? Give your answers in pence.

Red [   ]   Yellow [   ]   Purple [   ]

Write the ratio below as simply as possible.

270:180:45 [   ]

A popular games website for children has 3.8 million users in the ratio of three boys to five girls. How many boys and girls use the website?

Boys [   ]   Girls [   ]

What is the perimeter of
this compound shape?

28 cm

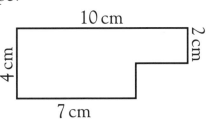

10 + 2 + 3 + 2 + 7 + 4 = 28

What is the perimeter of this regular hexagon?

7.68 cm

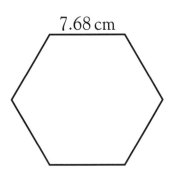

The perimeter of this regular pentagon is 625 m.
Calculate the length of each of its sides.

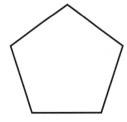

A square has an area of 625 cm². What is its perimeter?

The football pitch at Trentwood Sports Academy measures 110 m by 80 m. If the groundsman takes 10 minutes to mark a 20-m line, how long will it take him to mark the perimeter of the football pitch? Give your answer in hours and minutes.

A rectangle has a perimeter of 18 m. If the length of the rectangle measures 6.5 m, what is its width?

★ Area problems

A square sheet of paper has sides measuring 6 cm. A smaller square of sides 2 cm is cut out and removed from the sheet. What is the area of the shape that remains?

32 cm²

What is the area of this compound shape?

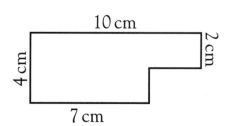

Calculate the area of this shape.

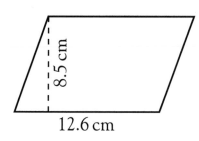

What is the area of this compound shape?

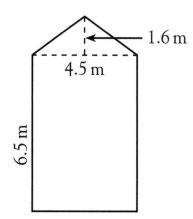

A rectangle has an area of 60 cm². Give six possible whole-number combinations for the length and width of the rectangle's sides.

What is the volume of this cube?
Hint: The volume of a cube is found using the formula a^3, where a represents the length of each edge.

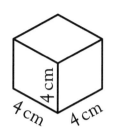

Volume of cube = a^3

so 4 x 4 x 4 = 64

64 cm³

Rhona has a jewellery box in the shape of a cuboid. It is 10 cm long, 4 cm wide and 3 cm high. Calculate its volume.

What is the volume of this cuboid?

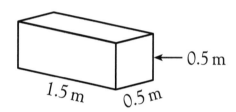

0.5 m

1.5 m   0.5 m

The edges of a cube are 2.5 m. What is its volume?

What is the volume of this cube?

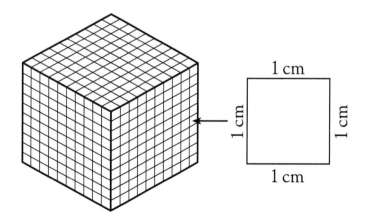

1 cm

1 cm   1 cm   1 cm

1 cm

A cuboid has a square base and its height is 20 cm. The volume of the cuboid is 720 cm³. What is the length of the sides of the base?

Mia has a playroom in her house for her children. The length, width and height of the room are 6 m, 5 m and 3 m respectively. Find the volume of the room.

Volume of cuboid = length x width x height

6 x 5 x 3 = 90

90 m³

A small fish tank is 40 cm long, 20 cm wide and 20 cm high and is filled with water up to three-quarters of its height. Calculate the volume of the water in the tank.

A cube has edges that are 3 cm long. If the length of the edges are doubled to make another cube, what is the difference in volume between the two cubes?

If the volume of a cube is 1 000 m³, what is the length of its edges?

The mass of a cube is 192 kg. If 1 cm³ of the cube has a mass of 3 g, what is the length of its edges?

Two edges of a cuboid measure 3 m and 4 m. The volume of the cuboid is 6 m³. Calculate the length of the third edge.

The volume of a cuboid is 60 cm³. Give three different sets of dimensions (length, width and height) possible for the cuboid.

For a science experiment, a chemical needs to be cooled down to –56°C. After an hour of freezing, the chemical's temperature fell to –29°C. How much further does the temperature still need to drop?

The difference between –56 and –29 is the same as

56 – 29 = 27

27°C

A mine shaft goes down 0.23 km. The first level of the mine lies 0.13 km down the shaft. What is the distance between the first level and the bottom of the shaft?

Two brothers, Logan and Harlow, had £185 in their joint bank account. Logan took out £112 from the account to buy a phone and Harlow took out £96 for a digital camera. By how much is the account now overdrawn?

During one day in Glasgow, the temperature varied from –2.8°C to 7.3°C. What was the difference in temperature?

Freshwater freezes at 0°C. Sea water, however, freezes at –2°C because of the salt in it. What is the difference in their freezing points?

One winter in a town in northeast Siberia, the average temperature was –31°C. The next winter, however, the average temperature dropped to –50°C. Calculate the difference between the two average temperatures.

Conversion problems

Petrol used to be measured in gallons rather than litres. If your grandfather had put 12 gallons of petrol in his car in the 1960s, what would that now be in litres? **Hint:** 1 gallon equals 4.55 l.

12 gallons = 12 x 4.55
= 54.6 litres

54.6 l

A chef's special pudding recipe requires 1.05 l of milk. Her measuring jug, however, is only marked in millilitres. Can you help the chef use the right amount of milk by converting 1.05 l to millilitres?

Each year, Jonah's parents measure his height. They record it in metres. Jonah is now 1.27 m tall. Convert his height to feet and inches. **Hint:** 1 inch equals 2.54 cm, and there are 12 inches in 1 foot.

A marathon is a 26.2-mile race. If one mile equals 1.6 km, calculate the distance of a marathon in kilometres.

How many years are the same as 3.6 decades?

[   ] years

On a recent visit to New York, Liam bought some souvenirs for his relatives. They cost him $21. How much will that be in pounds? **Note:** Find the most recent exchange rate between the US dollar and pound.

If **s** = **p** x **r**, where **p** is 3 and **r** is 4, calculate **s**.

$$s = p \times r$$
$$s = 3 \times 4$$
$$= 12$$

12

The area (**a**) of a triangle is found by multiplying the length of its base (**b**) by its height (**h**) and dividing by two. The formula is written as **a** = $\frac{1}{2}$**b** x **h** or $\frac{1}{2}$ **bh**.

The base of a triangle is 6 cm and its height is 8 cm. Use the formula to find its area.

The height of a triangle is 7.5 cm and its base is 5.9 cm. Find the area of the triangle.

If the base of a triangle is 6 cm and its area is 12 cm², what is the triangle's height?

The area of a triangle is 18 cm² and its height is 4 cm. What is the length of its base?

Three different numbers are represented by **a**, **b** and **c**.

If **a** = 4, **b** = 5 and **c** = 10, what is $a^2 + b^2 + c^2$?

If **a** = **b** + **c** and **a** = 9 and **c** = 2.5, what is **b**?

If **a** = b^2 and **a** = 36, what is **b**?

If **a** = $\frac{b}{c}$ where **a** is 12 and **b** is 48, what is **c**?

If $a = b - c$, where a is 14 and c is 9, find the value of b.

| 23 |

$$a = b - c$$
$$14 = b - 9$$
$$b = 14 + 9$$
$$= 23$$

Using the formula $a = b^2 + c$, solve the questions.

If b is 4 and c is 1, what is a?

When a is 14 and c is 5, what is b?

If c is 10 and a is 154, what is b?

What is a, when b is 1 and c is 0?

Using the formula, $x = \frac{y}{2} - 3$, solve the questions.

If x is 0, what is the value of y?

If y is 12, what is the value of x?

If y is 20, what is the value of x?

If x is $\frac{1}{2}$, what is the value of y?

A survey asked 30 children in Hampshire which football team they supported. Look at the chart to see the results. Then answer the questions below.

Favourite football teams

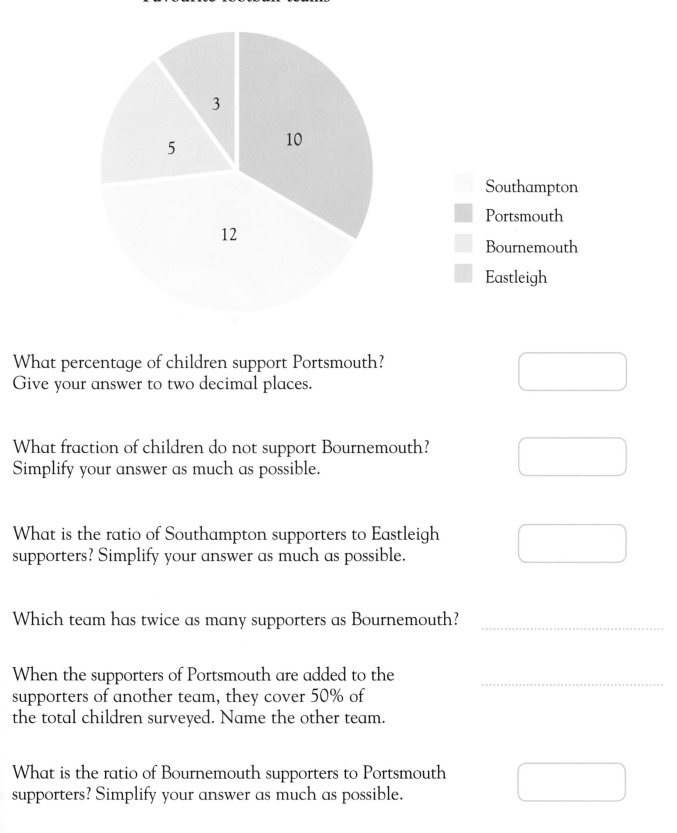

Southampton
Portsmouth
Bournemouth
Eastleigh

What percentage of children support Portsmouth? Give your answer to two decimal places.

What fraction of children do not support Bournemouth? Simplify your answer as much as possible.

What is the ratio of Southampton supporters to Eastleigh supporters? Simplify your answer as much as possible.

Which team has twice as many supporters as Bournemouth? ....

When the supporters of Portsmouth are added to the supporters of another team, they cover 50% of the total children surveyed. Name the other team. ....

What is the ratio of Bournemouth supporters to Portsmouth supporters? Simplify your answer as much as possible.

A survey of schoolchildren in Barnes, London, asked 100 boys and 100 girls where they would most like to spend a holiday when given four choices. Look at the chart to see their responses. Then answer the questions below.

Holiday destinations chosen by 200 children

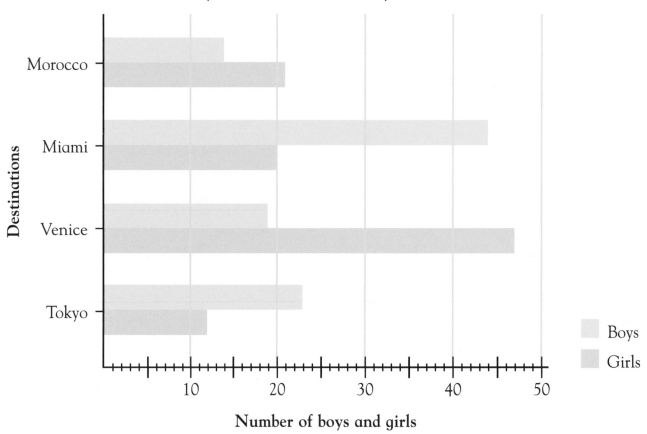

Number of boys and girls

What percentage of children selected Tokyo?

Which destination had the most similar number of votes between the boys and girls?

How many girls preferred Venice to Miami?

What percentage of boys did not select Venice?

Which destination was the most popular choice?

What percentage of children selected Venice?

Henning's cake recipe requires 0.15 kg of butter for each half kilogram of flour. If Henning uses 3 kg of flour, how much butter will he need?

0.9 kg

There are six half kilograms of flour in 3 kg.

So for the butter,
0.15 x 6 = 0.9

A gaming company increased the price of its latest computer game by 20% after it became a bestseller. If the new price is £54, what was the original price?

Out of 1 200 passengers on a cruise liner, 900 are over the age of 40 and the rest are below the age of 40. Calculate the ratio of passengers over 40 to those below 40. Write the ratio in its simplest form.

The area of a square is 64 m². If the length of each side of the square is doubled, what will be the area of the new square?

It took Quentin 4 hours 15 minutes to travel from Fleetwood to Bracknell. On the return journey, he took a slightly different route that was quicker by 20 minutes. How long was Quentin's return journey? Give your answer in hours and minutes.

Out of 60 goals scored in the Brentwood School Football Tournament, eight were penalties. What percentage of the goals were not penalties? Give your answer to two decimal places.

The perimeter (**P**) of a netball court is 91.5 m.
If the length (**l**) of the court is 30.5 m, what is
its width (**w**)?

15.25 m

$$P = 2(l + w)$$
$$91.5 = 2(30.5 + w)$$
$$91.5 = 61 + 2w$$
$$2w = 91.5 - 61$$
$$2w = 30.5$$
$$w = 15.25$$

The population of an island is 1.76 million. Of this number, 86% of the people were born on the island, while the rest came from outside and settled there. How many people were not born on the island?

people

The film *Adventure on the Atlantis* was released in the year MMII.
Write the year in numbers.

Before going to work, Audrey filled her car with 25 l of petrol.
If the cost of petrol was £1.29 per litre and Audrey paid with
four £10 notes, how much change did she receive?

A box of assorted muffins contains walnut, chocolate and blueberry muffins.
Three-eighths of the muffins in the box are blueberry and a quarter of them
are walnut. What fraction of the muffins are chocolate?

The perimeter of a rectangle is 45 m. If the length of the
rectangle is twice its width, what are the sides of the rectangle?

Length   Width

Ms Li's class has 45 pupils, 18 of which enjoy roller-coaster rides when they go to an amusement park. What fraction of pupils in her class do not enjoy roller-coaster rides? Simplify the fraction as far as possible.

$45 - 18 = 27$

$27 \div 45 = 0.6$

$0.6 = \dfrac{3}{5}$

$\boxed{\dfrac{3}{5}}$

Harlow, Tabitha and Scout share a flat in Birmingham. If they divide their monthly rent of £690 equally, how much rent does each pay in a year?

[ ]

Supreme Cakes Company baked a birthday cake that weighed 4.68 kg before the icing was added. The icing added an extra 15% to the weight of the cake. What is the new weight of the cake?

[ ]

The temperature difference between two towns in Slovakia is 8.5°C. If the town with the warmer temperature is 3.7°C, calculate the temperature of the colder town.

[ ]

The number of people at a Portsmouth football match is 18 450. Four-fifths of them are Portsmouth supporters and the rest support the away team. How many supporters does the away team have?

[ ] supporters

The area of a rectangle is 32 cm² and its perimeter is 24 cm. What are the rectangle's dimensions?

[ ]   [ ]

The distance between London and New York is 3 459 miles. If 1 mile = 1.6 km, calculate the distance to the nearest kilometre.

1 mile = 1.6 km

3 459 x 1.6

= 5 534.4

Round down to 5 534

5 534 km

During the interval of a film, Emerson received nine text messages, including three from his mother. What percentage of Emerson's messages were not from his mother? Give your answer to two decimal places.

Jack diluted a disinfectant in the ratio of one part disinfectant to eight parts water. If he used 25 ml of disinfectant, what was the total volume of the disinfectant and water mixture?

Sage works the night shift at a power station. Her shift starts at 23:30 and ends at 06:30. How long is it?

The end credits of a very old black-and-white television series showed that it was made in the year MCMXLIX. Write the year in numbers.

A three-bedroom house in London was sold for £870 000. A similar house in Swansea was sold at one-third of that price. How much was the house in Swansea sold for?

Each month, Dan uses 40% of his wage to pay off the mortgage on his house. If Dan earns £5 600 per month, how much money does he pay on the mortgage each year?

$\frac{40}{100}$ x 5 600

= 2 240

2 240 x 12

= 26 880

£26 880

Hannah organised a dinner party. She put three tables end to end to make one big table 6 m in length. The length of one of the smaller tables was 1.8 m and the other two were the same length as each other. Calculate the length of each of the other tables.

What is the area of the compound shape?

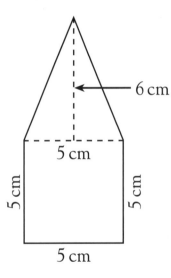

6 cm

5 cm

5 cm

5 cm

5 cm

Troy bought petrol at £1.30 per litre and paid with a £20 note. If he bought 12.5 l of petrol, how much change should he expect?

What is the volume (**V**) of a cuboid of length (**l**) 7.4 cm, width (**w**) 4.5 cm and height (**h**) 12 cm to the nearest cm³? Use the formula **V** = **l** x **w** x **h** or **V** = **lwh** to find the answer.

The signboard over the doorway of a shop is an isosceles triangle in shape. If the base of the triangle is 4.8 m and its height is 2.4 m, calculate its area.

Area = $\frac{1}{2}$ base x height

$\frac{1}{2}$ x 4.8 x 2.4

= 5.76

5.76 m²

The perimeter of a regular octagon is 116 cm. What is the length of each side?

A big packet of mixed nuts weighs 1.2 kg and 15% of the nuts are walnuts. How much do the walnuts weigh?

Hugh needs to perform a chemical experiment in a container at a temperature of –108°C. If the temperature in the container is 18.5°C, by how much will the temperature need to drop before the experiment can take place?

The surface area of a cube is found using the formula $6a^2$, where **a** is the length of each edge. If the length of each edge is 7.5 cm, what is the cube's total surface area?

Tahira is travelling from England to the United States and wants to exchange £400 for US dollars. If £1 has the same value as $1.56, how many dollars will Tahira get after the currency exchange?

An estate agent sold a house for £286 000 and earned a commission of 1.25% on the sale. How much money did she make?

$\frac{1.25}{100}$ x 286 000

= 3 575

£3 575

List the prime numbers between 40 and 50.

There is only one prime number between 90 and 100. What is it?

How much is 2% of 5% of £100?

A rectangle has sides that measure 12 cm and 3 cm. What will be the length of the sides of a square that has the same area as the rectangle?

After paying tax at the rate of 20%, Rhys has £1 440 left in his bank account. How much did Rhys have originally?

One of the tallest buildings in the world, the Tokyo Skytree, is 634 m high. An architect is planning a new building 5% taller than the Tokyo Skytree. How high will the new building be?

One-third of a wheat crop was sold to a local company and three-fifths to a large national firm. What fraction of the crop was not sold?

$\frac{1}{15}$

$$\frac{1}{3} + \frac{3}{5} + x = 1$$
$$x = 1 - (\frac{1}{3} + \frac{3}{5})$$
$$x = 1 - (\frac{5}{15} + \frac{9}{15})$$
$$x = \frac{1}{15}$$

A deli owner worked out the total cost of making a sandwich. The ratio of sandwich contents to labour needed to make one sandwich came out as 3:2. If the total cost of the sandwich is £1.80, what is the cost of the contents and what is the cost of labour?

Cost of contents [ ]   Cost of labour [ ]

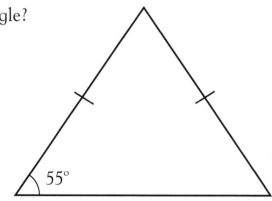

Which regular polygon has eight lines of symmetry?

[ ]

What is the next number in the sequence 3, 6, 10, 15?

[ ]

If $a = 4$ and $b = 7$, what is the value of $3(b - a)$?

[ ]

What are the missing angles of this isosceles triangle?

[ ]   [ ]

55°

The scores of four players on a computer game are 4 199, 2 805, 3 051 and 9 534 points. What is their combined total?

4 199 + 2 805 + 3 051 + 9 534

= 19 589

| 19 589 | points

What is the next number in the sequence 1, 4, 9, 16?

If three angles of a quadrilateral are 76°, 115° and 42°, what is the fourth angle?

Mr Richardson shared out 2 658 badges equally among 132 pupils in his maths classes. How many badges did each pupil receive and how many were left over?

Badges received by each pupil   Badges left over

A length of road needs resurfacing. It is divided into five equal parts for five engineering teams to work on. If the road is 18.6 miles long, what length is assigned to each team?

What are the common factors of 16 and 40?

Which two prime numbers lie between 80 and 90?

What is the first prime number after 109?

A steel girder is 8.454 m long. If four such girders are laid end to end, what will be their total length?

8.454 x 4

= 33.816

33.816 m

The cube of a number is 27. What is the original number?

Which factors of 36 are also multiples of six?

A square bedside table has sides measuring 20 cm. A larger square bedside table has sides twice as long. What is the difference in area of the two tables?

How many weeks and days are there in a 365-day year?

weeks   day(s)

A rectangle has a length of 9.3 cm and a width of 6.4 cm. Find out the perimeter of the rectangle using the formula 2(l + w), where l is length and w is width.

Which of these two equations is larger and by how much?
(8 + 4) x 6 or 8 + (4 x 6)

If $\frac{4}{5}$ of a number is 48, what is the number?	$\frac{4}{5}$ of $x = 48$
60	$4x = 5 \times 48 = 240$ $x = 240 \div 4 = 60$

Which factor of 50, other than 1, is also a square number?

Which number comes halfway between 3.846 and 1.994?

Find the perimeter of a rectangle with sides 11.23 cm and 8.92 cm.

If the cube of a number is 1, what is the original number?

Insert brackets into this equation so that the answer is 108.

$60 - 6 \times 2 = 108$

Use common denominators to work out which of these fractions is larger.

$\frac{2}{3}$ or $\frac{3}{5}$

Which two prime numbers give a product of 91?

If the perimeter (**P**) of a rectangle is 44.6 cm and
its width (**w**) is 9.6 cm, what is its length (**l**)?

12.7 cm

$$P = 2 (l + w)$$
$$44.6 = 2 (l + 9.6)$$
$$44.6 = 2l + 19.2$$
$$2l = 44.6 - 19.2$$
$$2l = 25.4$$
$$l = 12.7$$

Insert brackets into this equation so that the answer is 29.

8 + 7 x 3

Use common denominators to work out which of these fractions is smaller.

$\frac{9}{10}$ or $\frac{11}{12}$

Write the answer to 68 ÷ 5 in the following forms:

mixed fraction   decimal

quotient and remainder

Seven-tenths of an amount is £126. What is the whole amount?

The cube of a number is 125. What is the number?

What is the area of this parallelogram?

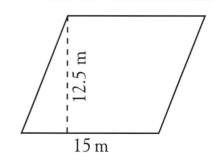

12.5 m

15 m

Answer section with parents' notes

Key Stage 2
Ages 9–11

This eight-page section provides answers and explanatory notes to all the problems in this book, enabling you to assess your child's work.

Work through each page together and ensure that your child understands each maths problem. Point out any mistakes your child makes and correct the errors. Your child should use the methods of working out taught at his or her school. In addition to making corrections, it is very important to praise your child's efforts and achievements.

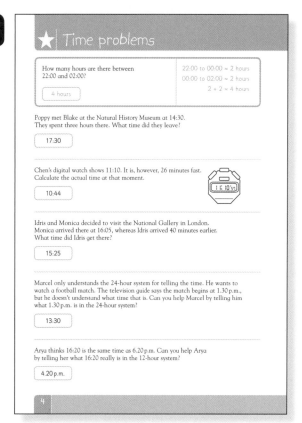

★ Time problems

How many hours are there between 22:00 and 02:00?	22:00 to 00:00 = 2 hours
4 hours	00:00 to 02:00 = 2 hours
	2 + 2 = 4 hours

Poppy met Blake at the Natural History Museum at 14:30. They spent three hours there. What time did they leave?

17:30

Chen's digital watch shows 11:10. It is, however, 26 minutes fast. Calculate the actual time at that moment.

10:44

Idris and Monica decided to visit the National Gallery in London. Monica arrived there at 16:05, whereas Idris arrived 40 minutes earlier. What time did Idris get there?

15:25

Marcel only understands the 24-hour system for telling the time. He wants to watch a football match. The television guide says the match begins at 1.30 p.m., but he doesn't understand what time that is. Can you help Marcel by telling him what 1.30 p.m. is in the 24-hour system?

13:30

Arya thinks 16:20 is the same time as 6.20 p.m. Can you help Arya by telling her what 16:20 really is in the 12-hour system?

4.20 p.m.

Ensure that your child is familiar with the 24-hour system. Introduce her to the later times, such as 22:00 and 23:30, because she will not normally be awake at these hours and so will not see digital times on devices.

Roman numerals ★

Dakota read in her history book that the Great Fire of London happened in the year MDCLXVI. Help Dakota write the year in numbers.	M = 1000, D = 500, C = 100, L = 50, X = 10, V = 5 and I = 1
1666	1000 + 500 + 100 + 50 + 10 + 5 + 1 = 1666

Using Roman numerals, write the number that is 10 more than each of these.

V [XV]   VIII [XVIII]   XLV [LV]

Write each of these years using Roman numerals.

2014 [MMXIV]   2002 [MMII]   1918 [MCMXVIII]

A farmer counted his two flocks of sheep one morning. One flock had DXII sheep and the other had D. How many sheep does the farmer have altogether? Write your answer in Roman numerals.

MXII sheep

In her maths exam, Greta had to solve this sum and write the answer in Roman numerals. What should she have written?

MDI + MCL = MMDCLI

The year before last, the population of a small town was MDV. Last year, however, the population went down by DL. Calculate the new population of the town and write the answer in Roman numerals.

CMLV

Some numbers can be written in more than one way with Roman numerals. For example, IV (4) can also be written as IIII. Also, when a smaller value precedes a larger value, as in IX (9), the smaller number is subtracted from the larger one.

★ Money problems

The cost of laying a garden patio is £48 per square metre. If the area of the patio is 8 m², what will be the total cost of laying it?	40 × 8 = 320
£384	8 × 8 = 64
	320 + 64 = 384

Emerson's trip to France is going to cost him £660. He has, however, saved only a third of that amount so far. How much more money does Emerson need to save for his trip?

£440

Lauren participated in a sponsored run for her favourite charity. She asked people to sponsor her 50 p for every kilometre she runs. Ten people sponsored her and she raised a total of £70. How many kilometres did Lauren run?

14 km

Four different coins make a total of 82 p. What are the coins?

50 p   20 p   10 p   2 p

Each month, Scarlett puts away a quarter of her wage as savings. If she earns £1 600 a month, how much money does she spend?

£1 200

It costs Eddy £380 to get his car repaired at his local garage. A fifth of the cost is for new car parts and the rest goes towards labour charges. How much do the parts cost and how much does the labour cost?

Cost of parts £76   Cost of labour £304

Including units in each step of the working out of a problem is useful when you need to convert from one unit to another, such as pounds to pence. Even if you don't use units in working out, always include them in your final answers.

Decimals, fractions & percentages 1 ★

Which decimal amount is the same as seven-eighths?

0.875

$\frac{1}{8} \approx 0.125$

$\frac{7}{8} \approx 7 \times 0.125$

≈ 0.875

At Clement Academy, maths lessons take up 0.2 of the school week. If a school week is 20 hours, how much time does the academy devote to subjects other than maths?

16 hours

Three-fifths of £18 is spent on a cinema ticket and 0.4 of the remainder on sweets. How much money is left after buying the ticket and the sweets?

£4.32

If 0.9 of a number is 63, what is the original number?

70

Akiko pays 20% tax on her monthly wage. If Akiko earns £1 680 a month, how much money will she have left after paying tax?

£1 344

A bookshop owner adds three-tenths to the price of each book he sells to a customer. If a new book costs the customer £15.60, how much did it cost the bookshop owner?

£12

The distance between Winchester and Walsall is 135 miles. Only 0.15 of the distance is motorway. What distance is not motorway?

114.75 miles

Make sure that your child understands the connection between fractions and decimals. He should be able to instantly convert the common fractions to their decimal equivalents and vice versa. For example, $\frac{3}{10} = 0.3$, $\frac{4}{5} = 0.8$ and $\frac{1}{8} = 0.125$.

★ Decimals, fractions & percentages 2

In a class of 20 pupils, seven have blond hair. What percentage is that?

35%

Percentage means "of 100"

$20 \approx \frac{1}{5} \times 100$

$7 \times 5 \approx 35$

7 out of 20 ≈ 35%

A mobile phone comes with 40 free apps already loaded. Five of these are quiz apps and four are music apps. What fraction of the free apps are neither quiz nor music apps?

$\frac{31}{40}$ apps

At a charity fundraiser, 1 000 lottery tickets are sold. The chance of winning with a ticket is 0.01. What is the maximum number of people who could win?

10 people

For their football album, Lou collected 46 football cards and Eve collected 34. What percentage of the total number of football cards did each collect?

Lou 57.5%   Eve 42.5%

An estate agent charges a commission of 1.25% of the selling price of each house. If a house is sold for £480 000, how much will the agent make as commission?

£6 000

Alexander has rented out his house for £900 a month. At the end of the first month, he spent two-fifteenths of the rent he was paid on repairs and kept the rest as profit. How much profit did he make that month?

£780

Encourage your child to practise converting fractions and decimals to their percentage equivalents. She should be able to instantly recall simple conversions, such as $\frac{7}{10}$ is 70% and 0.25 is 25%.

Decimals, fractions & percentages 3 ★

In one year, the price of petrol rose by 5%. If the original price was £1.20 per litre, what did it cost after the rise?

£1.26

5% of £1 ≈ £0.05

5% of 20p ≈ £0.01

1.20 + 0.05 + 0.01 ≈ 1.26

Write the percentage equivalent of these fractions.

$\frac{9}{10}$ 90% $\frac{4}{5}$ 80% $\frac{7}{20}$ 35%

Rowan practises for a marathon by running 12 km a day. A few days before the marathon, he increases the distance by 15%. Calculate the new distance Rowan runs.

13.8 km

In a school with 1 400 pupils, 45% have French classes and the rest study German. How many study each language?

French 630   German 770

A teacher needs to mark 40 exercise books in one evening. After three hours, he has marked 0.7 of them. How many books still need to be marked?

12 exercise books

A restaurant expects each customer to pay a 15% tip on his or her bill. If a meal at the restaurant costs £45, how much tip will a customer be expected to pay?

£6.75

A doctor has 4 800 registered patients. Last year, however, only 1 920 patients visited her. What percentage did not visit her last year?

60%

To make fractions, decimals and percentages easier for your child to understand, use day-to-day scenarios to explain them. Remind him that 1% of £1 is 1 p and 1% of 1 m is 1 cm. This will help make problems simpler and quicker to solve.

★ Ratio problems

A woodland has trees in the ratio of two oaks to seven elms. If there are 16 oak trees in the woodland, how many elm trees will there be?

56 elms

oak:elms ≈ 2:7

16 (oaks) ≈ 8 × 2

so number of elms ≈ 8 × 7

≈ 56

In a class of 30 children, six children bring packed lunches from home and the rest have school meals. What is the ratio of packed lunches to school meals? **Note:** Write the ratio as simply as possible.

1:4

The ratio of a school playground's length to its width is 5:4. If the area of the playground is 180 m², calculate its length and width.

Length 15 m   Width 12 m

In a packet of sweets, for every four red sweets there are two yellow sweets and one purple sweet. If the packet costs £1.12, how much does each type of sweet contribute towards the total cost? Give your answers in pence.

Red 64 p   Yellow 32 p   Purple 16 p

Write the ratio below as simply as possible.

270:180:45   6:4:1

A popular games website for children has 3.8 million users in the ratio of three boys to five girls. How many boys and girls use the website?

Boys 1 425 000   Girls 2 375 000

Ratios can be tricky to understand and can be easily confused with fractions. You can help your child understand ratios by using the scale on a map to work out together actual distances between cities or towns.

Perimeter problems ★

What is the perimeter of this compound shape?

28 cm

10 + 2 + 3 + 2 + 7 + 4 = 28

What is the perimeter of this regular hexagon?

46.08 cm

7.68 cm

The perimeter of this regular pentagon is 625 m. Calculate the length of each of its sides.

125 m

A square has an area of 625 cm². What is its perimeter?

100 cm

The football pitch at Trentwood Sports Academy measures 110 m by 80 m. If the groundsman takes 10 minutes to mark a 20-m line, how long will it take him to mark the perimeter of the football pitch? Give your answer in hours and minutes.

3 hours 10 minutes

A rectangle has a perimeter of 18 m. If the length of the rectangle measures 6.5 m, what is its width?

2.5 m

As an extra exercise, ask your child to work out the perimeter of household objects such as a rectangular table top or a book. Ask him to estimate the perimeters first and then measure them with a ruler or tape measure.

★ Area problems

A square sheet of paper has sides measuring 6 cm. A smaller square of sides 2 cm is cut out and removed from the sheet. What is the area of the shape that remains?

32 cm²

Area of the large square
6 x 6 = 36 cm²

Area of the smaller square
2 x 2 = 4 cm²

36 – 4 = 32

What is the area of this compound shape?

34 cm²

10 cm
4 cm
7 cm
2 cm

Calculate the area of this shape.

107.1 cm²

8.5 cm
12.6 cm

What is the area of this compound shape?

32.85 m²

1.6 m
4.5 m
6.5 m

A rectangle has an area of 60 cm². Give six possible whole-number combinations for the length and width of the rectangle's sides.

| 60 cm x 1 cm | 20 cm x 3 cm | 12 cm x 5 cm |
| 30 cm x 2 cm | 15 cm x 4 cm | 10 cm x 6 cm |

Children are usually taught two ways of writing units of area, for example, square centimetre and cm². Make sure your child always writes the unit of area using the format that is taught at her school.

Volume problems 1 ★

What is the volume of this cube?
Hint: The volume of a cube is found using the formula a³, where a represents the length of each edge.

64 cm³

Volume of cube = a³
so 4 x 4 x 4 = 64

4 cm
4 cm
4 cm

Rhona has a jewellery box in the shape of a cuboid. It is 10 cm long, 4 cm wide and 3 cm high. Calculate its volume.

120 cm³

What is the volume of this cuboid?

0.375 m³

0.5 m
1.5 m
0.5 m

The edges of a cube are 2.5 m. What is its volume?

15.625 m³

What is the volume of this cube?

1 000 cm³

1 cm
1 cm
1 cm
1 cm

A cuboid has a square base and its height is 20 cm. The volume of the cuboid is 720 cm³. What is the length of the sides of the base?

6 cm

Before working on problems on volume, make sure that your child has learned all the formulae needed and understood them. She needs to know that volume means the amount of space inside a shape.

★ Volume problems 2

Mia has a playroom in her house for her children. The length, width and height of the room are 6 m, 5 m and 3 m respectively. Find the volume of the room.

90 m³

Volume of cuboid = length x width x height
6 x 5 x 3 = 90

A small fish tank is 40 cm long, 20 cm wide and 20 cm high and is filled with water up to three-quarters of its height. Calculate the volume of the water in the tank.

12 000 cm³

A cube has edges that are 3 cm long. If the length of the edges are doubled to make another cube, what is the difference in volume between the two cubes?

189 cm³

If the volume of a cube is 1 000 m³, what is the length of its edges?

10 m

The mass of a cube is 192 kg. If 1 cm³ of the cube has a mass of 3 g, what is the length of its edges?

40 cm

Two edges of a cuboid measure 3 m and 4 m. The volume of the cuboid is 6 m³. Calculate the length of the third edge.

0.5 m

The volume of a cuboid is 60 cm³. Give three different sets of dimensions (length, width and height) possible for the cuboid. **Answers may vary**

| 1 cm x 2 cm x 30 cm | 2 cm x 5 cm x 6 cm | 15 cm x 4 cm x 1 cm |

At this age at school, your child will be working mainly with cubes and cuboids in maths volume problems. However, he should understand that volume applies to all 3-D shapes.

Negative amounts ★

For a science experiment, a chemical needs to be cooled down to –56°C. After an hour of freezing, the chemical's temperature fell to –29°C. How much further does the temperature still need to drop?

> The difference between –56 and –29 is the same as 56 – 29 = 27

27°C

A mine shaft goes down 0.23 km. The first level of the mine lies 0.13 km down the shaft. What is the distance between the first level and the bottom of the shaft?

0.1 km

Two brothers, Logan and Harlow, had £185 in their joint bank account. Logan took out £112 from the account to buy a phone and Harlow took out £96 for a digital camera. By how much is the account now overdrawn?

£23

During one day in Glasgow, the temperature varied from –2.8°C to 7.3°C. What was the difference in temperature?

10.1°C

Freshwater freezes at 0°C. Sea water, however, freezes at –2°C because of the salt in it. What is the difference in their freezing points?

2°C

One winter in a town in northeast Siberia, the average temperature was –31°C. The next winter, however, the average temperature dropped to –50°C. Calculate the difference between the two average temperatures.

19°C

Your child may not understand that you owe a bank money when your bank account is overdrawn or has a negative balance. Also, tell her that negative or minus temperatures are temperatures below 0°.

★ Conversion problems

Petrol used to be measured in gallons rather than litres. If your grandfather had put 12 gallons of petrol in his car in the 1960s, what would that now be in litres? **Hint:** 1 gallon equals 4.55 l.

> 12 gallons = 12 × 4.55 = 54.6 litres

54.6 l

A chef's special pudding recipe requires 1.05 l of milk. Her measuring jug, however, is only marked in millilitres. Can you help the chef use the right amount of milk by converting 1.05 l to millilitres?

1 050 ml

Each year, Jonah's parents measure his height. They record it in metres. Jonah is now 1.27 m tall. Convert his height to feet and inches. **Hint:** 1 inch equals 2.54 cm, and there are 12 inches in 1 foot.

4 feet 2 inches

A marathon is a 26.2-mile race. If one mile equals 1.6 km, calculate the distance of a marathon in kilometres.

41.92 km

How many years are the same as 3.6 decades?

36 years

On a recent visit to New York, Liam bought some souvenirs for his relatives. They cost him $21. How much will that be in pounds? **Note:** Find the most recent exchange rate between the US dollar and pound.

Answers may vary

Try introducing your child to different foreign currencies, such as the US dollar and the euro. Encourage him to find out the conversion rates of these currencies on the internet or in the finance section of a newspaper.

Simple formulae 1 ★

If $s = p \times r$, where p is 3 and r is 4, calculate s.

> $s = p \times r$
> $s = 3 \times 4$
> $= 12$

12

The area (a) of a triangle is found by multiplying the length of its base (b) by its height (h) and dividing by two. The formula is written as $a = \frac{1}{2} b \times h$ or $\frac{1}{2} bh$.

The base of a triangle is 6 cm and its height is 8 cm. Use the formula to find its area.

24 cm²

The height of a triangle is 7.5 cm and its base is 5.9 cm. Find the area of the triangle.

22.125 cm²

If the base of a triangle is 6 cm and its area is 12 cm², what is the triangle's height?

4 cm

The area of a triangle is 18 cm² and its height is 4 cm. What is the length of its base?

9 cm

Three different numbers are represented by a, b and c.

If $a = 4$, $b = 5$ and $c = 10$, what is $a^2 + b^2 + c^2$? · 141

If $a = b + c$ and $a = 9$ and $c = 2.5$, what is b? · 6.5

If $a = b^2$ and $a = 36$, what is b? · 6

If $a = \frac{b}{c}$ where a is 12 and b is 48, what is c? · 4

Simple formulae, as on this page, are a good introduction to algebra. The formulae may include a multiplication sign initially, for example, $a = b \times c$. At higher stages, the sign will not be used and it will be stated as $a = bc$.

★ Simple formulae 2

If $a = b - c$, where a is 14 and c is 9, find the value of b.

> $a = b - c$
> $14 = b - 9$
> $b = 14 + 9$
> $= 23$

23

Using the formula $a = b^2 + c$, solve the questions.

If b is 4 and c is 1, what is a? · 17

When a is 14 and c is 5, what is b? · 3

If c is 10 and a is 154, what is b? · 12

What is a, when b is 1 and c is 0? · 1

Using the formula $x = \frac{y}{2} - 3$, solve the questions.

If x is 0, what is the value of y? · 6

If y is 12, what is the value of x? · 3

If y is 20, what is the value of x? · 7

If x is $\frac{1}{2}$, what is the value of y? · 7

A simple formula is often written in the form $a = b + c$. Explain to your child that it can also be written in the form $x + y = z$ and that the sum total can be shown on either the left or the right.

Understanding charts 1 ★

A survey asked 30 children in Hampshire which football team they supported. Look at the chart to see the results. Then answer the questions below.

Favourite football teams

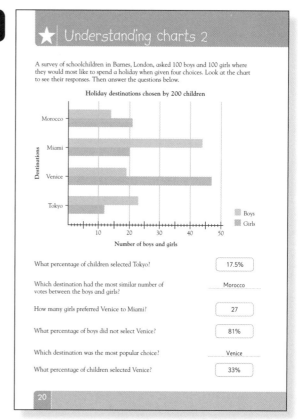

- Southampton
- Portsmouth
- Bournemouth
- Eastleigh

(pie segments labelled: 3, 10, 5, 12)

What percentage of children support Portsmouth?
Give your answer to two decimal places.
33.33%

What fraction of children do not support Bournemouth?
Simplify your answer as much as possible.
5/6

What is the ratio of Southampton supporters to Eastleigh supporters? Simplify your answer as much as possible.
4:1

Which team has twice as many supporters as Bournemouth?
Portsmouth

When the supporters of Portsmouth are added to the supporters of another team, they cover 50% of the total children surveyed. Name the other team.
Bournemouth

What is the ratio of Bournemouth supporters to Portsmouth supporters? Simplify your answer as much as possible.
1:2

Point out to your child the charts or graphs you come across in magazines and books or on food packaging. Discuss how good or bad they are at conveying information. Note how she interprets the results.

★ Understanding charts 2

A survey of schoolchildren in Barnes, London, asked 100 boys and 100 girls where they would most like to spend a holiday when given four choices. Look at the chart to see their responses. Then answer the questions below.

Holiday destinations chosen by 200 children

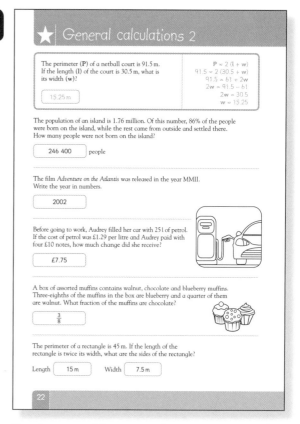

Destinations: Morocco, Miami, Venice, Tokyo
Number of boys and girls

- Boys
- Girls

What percentage of children selected Tokyo?
17.5%

Which destination had the most similar number of votes between the boys and girls?
Morocco

How many girls preferred Venice to Miami?
27

What percentage of boys did not select Venice?
81%

Which destination was the most popular choice?
Venice

What percentage of children selected Venice?
33%

Work with your child to create data charts, such as pie charts and bar charts. While drawing these, show him that the most important thing about a chart is the clarity of the information displayed.

General calculations 1 ★

Henning's cake recipe requires 0.15 kg of butter for each half kilogram of flour. If Henning uses 3 kg of flour, how much butter will he need?
0.9 kg

There are six half kilograms of flour in 3 kg.

So for the butter,
0.15 × 6 = 0.9

A gaming company increased the price of its latest computer game by 20% after it became a bestseller. If the new price is £54, what was the original price?
£45

Out of 1 200 passengers on a cruise liner, 900 are over the age of 40 and the rest are below the age of 40. Calculate the ratio of passengers over 40 to those below 40. Write the ratio in its simplest form.
3:1

The area of a square is 64 m². If the length of each side of the square is doubled, what will be the area of the new square?
256 m²

It took Quentin 4 hours 15 minutes to travel from Fleetwood to Bracknell. On the return journey, he took a slightly different route that was quicker by 20 minutes. How long was Quentin's return journey? Give your answer in hours and minutes.
3 hours 55 minutes

Out of 60 goals scored in the Brentwood School Football Tournament, eight were penalties. What percentage of the goals were not penalties? Give your answer to two decimal places.
86.67%

This page has a mix of various kinds of maths problem. Many of the calculations needed can be solved quickly using a calculator. However, at this stage, your child should be encouraged to solve the problems without one.

★ General calculations 2

The perimeter (P) of a netball court is 91.5 m. If the length (l) of the court is 30.5 m, what is its width (w)?
15.25 m

$$P = 2 (l + w)$$
$$91.5 = 2 (30.5 + w)$$
$$91.5 = 61 + 2w$$
$$2w = 91.5 - 61$$
$$2w = 30.5$$
$$w = 15.25$$

The population of an island is 1.76 million. Of this number, 86% of the people were born on the island, while the rest came from outside and settled there. How many people were not born on the island?
246 400 people

The film *Adventure on the Atlantis* was released in the year MMII. Write the year in numbers.
2002

Before going to work, Audrey filled her car with 25 l of petrol. If the cost of petrol was £1.29 per litre and Audrey paid with four £10 notes, how much change did she receive?
£7.75

A box of assorted muffins contains walnut, chocolate and blueberry muffins. Three-eighths of the muffins in the box are blueberry and a quarter of them are walnut. What fraction of the muffins are chocolate?
3/8

The perimeter of a rectangle is 45 m. If the length of the rectangle is twice its width, what are the sides of the rectangle?
Length **15 m** Width **7.5 m**

Reading a problem more than once is a good way of understanding it clearly without missing important details. Your child can highlight the important aspects of the problem with a marker pen while reading it.

General calculations 3 ⭐

Ms Li's class has 45 pupils, 18 of which enjoy roller-coaster rides when they go to an amusement park. What fraction of pupils in her class do not enjoy roller-coaster rides? Simplify the fraction as far as possible.

$45 - 18 = 27$
$27 \div 45 = 0.6$
$0.6 = \frac{3}{5}$

$\boxed{\frac{3}{5}}$

Harlow, Tabitha and Scout share a flat in Birmingham. If they divide their monthly rent of £690 equally, how much rent does each pay in a year?

$\boxed{£2\ 760}$

Supreme Cakes Company baked a birthday cake that weighed 4.68 kg before the icing was added. The icing added an extra 15% to the weight of the cake. What is the new weight of the cake?

$\boxed{5.382\ kg}$

The temperature difference between two towns in Slovakia is 8.5°C. If the town with the warmer temperature is 3.7°C, calculate the temperature of the colder town.

$\boxed{-4.8°C}$

The number of people at a Portsmouth football match is 18 450. Four-fifths of them are Portsmouth supporters and the rest support the away team. How many supporters does the away team have?

$\boxed{3\ 690}$ supporters

The area of a rectangle is 32 cm² and its perimeter is 24 cm. What are the rectangle's dimensions?

$\boxed{8\ cm}$ $\boxed{4\ cm}$

Encourage your child to work out parts of problems mentally whenever she can. For more complex problems, ask her to write down the numbers in clear handwriting. This approach will make it easier for her to solve problems.

⭐ General calculations 4

The distance between London and New York is 3 459 miles. If 1 mile = 1.6 km, calculate the distance to the nearest kilometre.

1 mile ≈ 1.6 km
$3\ 459 \times 1.6$
$\approx 5\ 534.4$
Round down to 5 534

$\boxed{5\ 534\ km}$

During the interval of a film, Emerson received nine text messages, including three from his mother. What percentage of Emerson's messages were not from his mother? Give your answer to two decimal places.

$\boxed{66.67\%}$

Jack diluted a disinfectant in the ratio of one part disinfectant to eight parts water. If he used 25 ml of disinfectant, what was the total volume of the disinfectant and water mixture?

$\boxed{225\ ml}$

Sage works the night shift at a power station. Her shift starts at 23:30 and ends at 06:30. How long is it?

$\boxed{7\ hours}$

The end credits of a very old black-and-white television series showed that it was made in the year MCMXLIX. Write the year in numbers.

$\boxed{1949}$

A three-bedroom house in London was sold for £870 000. A similar house in Swansea was sold at one-third of that price. How much was the house in Swansea sold for?

$\boxed{£290\ 000}$

After finishing the problems on each page, encourage your child to get into the habit of going through each problem again to double-check the answers and correct any mistakes he may have made.

General calculations 5 ⭐

Each month, Dan uses 40% of his wage to pay off the mortgage on his house. If Dan earns £5 600 per month, how much money does he pay on the mortgage each year?

$\frac{40}{100} \times 5\ 600$
$= 2\ 240$
$2\ 240 \times 12$
$= 26\ 880$

$\boxed{£26\ 880}$

Hannah organised a dinner party. She put three tables end to end to make one big table 6 m in length. The length of one of the smaller tables was 1.8 m and the other two were the same length as each other. Calculate the length of each of the other tables.

$\boxed{2.1\ m}$

What is the area of the compound shape?

$\boxed{40\ cm^2}$

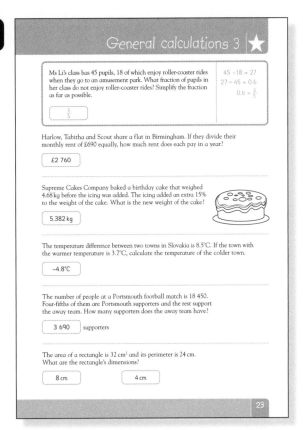

6 cm
5 cm
5 cm
5 cm
5 cm

Troy bought petrol at £1.30 per litre and paid with a £20 note. If he bought 12.5 l of petrol, how much change should he expect?

$\boxed{£3.75}$

What is the volume (**V**) of a cuboid of length (**l**) 7.4 cm, width (**w**) 4.5 cm and height (**h**) 12 cm to the nearest cm³? Use the formula **V = l x w x h** or **V = lwh** to find the answer.

$\boxed{400\ cm^3}$

By this time, your child should be able to read a problem and sort out which operations will be needed to solve it. She should work out the problem accurately and check to see if the answer is sensible.

⭐ General calculations 6

The signboard over the doorway of a shop is an isosceles triangle in shape. If the base of the triangle is 4.8 m and its height is 2.4 m, calculate its area.

Area = $\frac{1}{2}$ base x height
$\frac{1}{2} \times 4.8 \times 2.4$
$= 5.76$

$\boxed{5.76\ m^2}$

The perimeter of a regular octagon is 116 cm. What is the length of each side?

$\boxed{14.5\ cm}$

A big packet of mixed nuts weighs 1.2 kg and 15% of the nuts are walnuts. How much do the walnuts weigh?

$\boxed{0.18\ kg}$

Hugh needs to perform a chemical experiment in a container at a temperature of −108°C. If the temperature in the container is 18.5°C, by how much will the temperature need to drop before the experiment can take place?

$\boxed{126.5°C}$

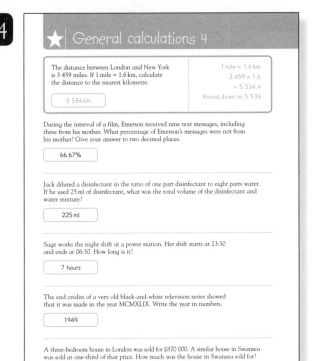

The surface area of a cube is found using the formula 6a², where a is the length of each edge. If the length of each edge is 7.5 cm, what is the cube's total surface area?

$\boxed{337.5\ cm^2}$

Tahira is travelling from England to the United States and wants to exchange £400 for US dollars. If £1 has the same value as $1.56, how many dollars will Tahira get after the currency exchange?

$\boxed{\$624}$

Children often make the mistake of reading questions in a rush. Make sure that your child looks closely at the numbers and does not make careless assumptions about what is being asked in the question.

Harder problems 1 ★

An estate agent sold a house for £286 000 and earned a commission of 1.25% on the sale. How much money did she make?

$\frac{1.25}{100} \times 286\,000$

$= 3\,575$

£3 575

List the prime numbers between 40 and 50.

41   43   47

There is only one prime number between 90 and 100. What is it?

97

How much is 2% of 5% of £100?

10 p

A rectangle has sides that measure 12 cm and 3 cm. What will be the length of the sides of a square that has the same area as the rectangle?

6 cm

After paying tax at the rate of 20%, Rhys has £1 440 left in his bank account. How much did Rhys have originally?

£1 800

One of the tallest buildings in the world, the Tokyo Skytree, is 634 m high. An architect is planning a new building 5% taller than the Tokyo Skytree. How high will the new building be?

665.7 m

As your child progresses in maths, speed is as important as accuracy. So before he moves on to harder problems, such as the ones given on this page, encourage him to master the basic operations and topics covered in this book.

★ Harder problems 2

One-third of a wheat crop was sold to a local company and three-fifths to a large national firm. What fraction of the crop was not sold?

$\frac{1}{3} + \frac{3}{5} + x = 1$

$x = 1 - (\frac{1}{3} + \frac{3}{5})$

$x = 1 - (\frac{5}{15} + \frac{9}{15})$

$x = \frac{1}{15}$

$\frac{1}{15}$

A deli owner worked out the total cost of making a sandwich. The ratio of sandwich contents to labour needed to make one sandwich came out as 3:2. If the total cost of the sandwich is £1.80, what is the cost of the contents and what is the cost of labour?

Cost of contents   £1.08   Cost of labour   72 p

Which regular polygon has eight lines of symmetry?

Octagon

What is the next number in the sequence 3, 6, 10, 15?

21

If a = 4 and b = 7, what is the value of 3(b – a)?

9

What are the missing angles of this isosceles triangle?

70°   55°

55°

While your child is working on a problem, make a quick estimate of what the answer should be. When your child shows you the answer she has calculated, check it against your estimate to see if they roughly match.

Harder problems 3 ★

The scores of four players on a computer game are 4 199, 2 805, 3 051 and 9 534 points. What is their combined total?

$4\,199 + 2\,805 + 3\,051 + 9\,534$

$= 19\,589$

19 589   points

What is the next number in the sequence 1, 4, 9, 16?

25

If three angles of a quadrilateral are 76°, 115° and 42°, what is the fourth angle?

127°

Mr Richardson shared out 2 658 badges equally among 132 pupils in his maths classes. How many badges did each pupil receive and how many were left over?

Badges received by each pupil   20   Badges left over   18

A length of road needs resurfacing. It is divided into five equal parts for five engineering teams to work on. If the road is 18.6 miles long, what length is assigned to each team?

3.72 miles

What are the common factors of 16 and 40?

1   2   4   8

Which two prime numbers lie between 80 and 90?

83   89

What is the first prime number after 109?

113

Working on harder questions regularly will build your child's confidence in problem solving. Always check an answer in the context of the question to see if it is reasonable.

★ Harder problems 4

A steel girder is 8.454 m long. If four such girders are laid end to end, what will be their total length?

8.454×4

$= 33.816$

33.816 m

The cube of a number is 27. What is the original number?

3

Which factors of 36 are also multiples of six?

6   12   18   36

A square bedside table has sides measuring 20 cm. A larger square bedside table has sides twice as long. What is the difference in area of the two tables?

1 200 cm²

How many weeks and days are there in a 365-day year?

52   weeks   1   day(s)

A rectangle has a length of 9.3 cm and a width of 6.4 cm. Find out the perimeter of the rectangle using the formula 2(l + w), where l is length and w is width.

31.4 cm

Which of these two equations is larger and by how much?
(8 + 4) x 6 or 8 + (4 x 6)

(8 + 4) x 6 is larger by 40

If your child gets an answer wrong, encourage him to explain to you the method and operation(s) he used to solve the problem. If he cannot explain the method, it means that the concepts are still not clear to him.

Harder problems 5 ★

If $\frac{4}{5}$ of a number is 48, what is the number?

60	$\frac{4}{5}$ of x = 48 4x = 5 × 48 = 240 x = 240 ÷ 4 = 60

Which factor of 50, other than 1, is also a square number?

25

Which number comes halfway between 3.846 and 1.994?

2.92

Find the perimeter of a rectangle with sides 11.23 cm and 8.92 cm.

40.3 cm

If the cube of a number is 1, what is the original number?

1

Insert brackets into this equation so that the answer is 108.

60 – 6 × 2 = 108   (60 – 6) × 2 = 108

Use common denominators to work out which of these fractions is larger.

$\frac{2}{3}$ or $\frac{3}{5}$ $\frac{2}{3}$

Which two prime numbers give a product of 91?

7   13

By now, your child should be very familiar with the concepts of whole numbers, fractions and percentages and should be able to use them without difficulty in calculations.

★ Harder problems 6

If the perimeter (P) of a rectangle is 44.6 cm and its width (w) is 9.6 cm, what is its length (l)?

12.7 cm	P = 2 (l + w) 44.6 = 2 (l + 9.6) 44.6 = 2l + 19.2 2l = 44.6 – 19.2 2l = 25.4 l = 12.7

Insert brackets into this equation so that the answer is 29.

8 + 7 × 3   8 + (7 × 3)

Use common denominators to work out which of these fractions is smaller.

$\frac{9}{10}$ or $\frac{11}{12}$ $\frac{9}{10}$

Write the answer to 68 ÷ 5 in the following forms:

mixed fraction $13\frac{3}{5}$ decimal   13.6

quotient and remainder   13 and 3

Seven-tenths of an amount is £126. What is the whole amount?

£180

The cube of a number is 125. What is the number?

5

What is the area of this parallelogram?

187.5 m²

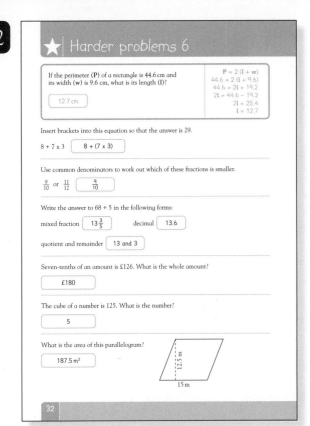

12.5 m

15 m

Make sure that your child knows that the numerator is the number at the top of the fraction and the denominator is the number at the bottom.